Con

Before you begin

What could be a happier occasion than a child's birthday party? You can make your child's party even more special with a unique birthday cake decorated by you! Each of the fabulous cakes in BIRTHDAY CAKES FOR KIDS is beautifully photographed and has easy-to-follow step-by-step directions.

The cakes are marked with one, two or three birthday candles to signify the time and skill needed. If you are a beginner, you may want to start with cakes marked with one candle. Then, as your confidence builds, move on to cakes with two or three candles. **Read through the following information before starting.** You will discover many helpful tips and important guidelines to make your cake decorating easier and more fun!

SPECIAL EQUIPMENT

The right equipment not only makes cake decorating easier but also gives more professional results. All of the equipment mentioned here is available in stores carrying cake decorating supplies.

Special Equipment (*clockwise from bottom left*): Assorted decorating tips, pastry bags, coupler, wooden picks and skewers, paste colors, cooling rack, pastry brush, cake comb, assorted spatulas.

Flexible metal spatulas of various sizes are useful in applying frosting. Use one with a narrow tip to get into small areas. A large flexible metal spatula makes smoothing the frosting on large flat areas easier.

Wooden picks and wooden or metal skewers are useful for marking designs and lines on the cakes.

Paste food colors are recommended for coloring the frosting as they do not thin the frosting like liquid colorings and they create bright, vibrant colors. For more information on coloring frosting see page 8.

A **pastry bag** with several tips is essential for piping decorations. The pastry bag can be a reusable bag, a plastic disposable bag or a bag folded from a parchment paper triangle. We recommend the following basic **decorating tips:** several sizes of writing tips (*numbers 3, 5, 9 and 12*), a star tip (*number 28*) and a basketweave tip (*number 47*). See page 10 for a photo and in-depth explanation of various decorating tips.

A **coupler** inserted into the pastry bag before filling makes changing tips easier. See page 9 for additional information on the coupler and how it is used.

An **icing comb** can be used to create lines and patterns in frosting (see page 58).

Cake boards are made of heavy cardboard and are used for cakes that are too large to fit on a plate or tray. See page 7 for instructions on how to cover cake boards.

BASIC CAKE KNOW-HOW
Cake Mixes vs. Cakes from Scratch
Using a packaged cake mix can save time, but be aware that cakes made from mixes are usually more tender and crumbly than cakes made from scratch. Place the cooled cake in the freezer for 30 to 45 minutes to firm cake for easier cutting, frosting and decorating.

If the birthday cake you choose has many small pieces that may be difficult to cut and frost, use one of the cake recipes on pages 92 and 93, or your own favorite recipe. Be sure to use a layer of Base Frosting (see page 94) to seal in the crumbs.

The Best Baking Pans
For great cakes, use shiny metal pans or pans with a nonstick finish. Grease and flour all pans before adding the cake batter. *Even nonstick pans should be lightly greased.* To grease a pan, spread a thin layer of vegetable shortening on the bottom and sides of the cake pan. Add a small amount of flour then tilt and shake the pan until flour covers the bottom and sides. Shake out any excess flour. *Or*, grease and line pan bottom with waxed paper (flouring the pan is unnecessary). See tip on page 5 about removing waxed paper liners.

Dividing the Batter
When baking layer cakes, it is important to divide the batter equally between the pans to make even layers. Either measure the batter and divide it equally (for example, 2 cups of batter in each pan) or weigh the pans after adding the batter. With practice, you will be able to judge by eye whether the batter in each pan is equal. Spread the batter evenly in the pans before baking.

Testing for Doneness

Always bake cakes at the oven temperature and time specified in the recipe. Test cakes after the shortest time given. A cake is done when a wooden pick inserted into the center comes out clean. It should pull away from the side of the pan and spring back when lightly touched in the center. White and yellow cakes should be lightly browned.

Cooling Cakes

Let cakes cool in the pan on a wire rack for about 10 minutes. Loosen cake edges with a spatula, place the rack, top-side down, over the pan. Flip the rack and the pan over together and the cake should drop out onto the rack. If it does not come out, tap the bottom of the pan; the cake should come out easily. Remove the pan. If using a waxed paper liner, carefully peel it off while the cake is still warm. Place a second wire rack over the cake and flip both racks and the cake back over so the cake can cool top-side up. Remove the top rack. If a cake is removed from the pan too soon, it may crack and break. If it is allowed to cool too long, it may stick to the pan. Always cool a cake completely before frosting.

Storing Cakes

Cool cakes completely before covering and storing. If using the undecorated layers within two days, wrap tightly in foil or plastic wrap and store in a cool place. For longer storage, wrap in heavy-duty foil or place in airtight freezer bags; freeze for up to two months. To thaw, remove the layers from the freezer and let them thaw, wrapped, at room temperature.

For storing decorated cakes, first set frosting and decorations by freezing unwrapped cake for 1 to 2 hours or until the frosting has hardened. Wrap tightly and freeze up to one month. Unwrap before thawing.

BEFORE FROSTING

Trimming Cakes

Trimmed cakes are easier to frost and give more professional results. For best results, use a serrated knife long enough to cut across the top in one stroke. Use a gentle sawing motion as you cut through the cake. The rounded tops of round, square and rectangular cakes should be trimmed to form a flat surface.

The sides of cakes that are square or rectangular should also be trimmed to make them more even.

Use a soft pastry brush to remove all loose cake crumbs. Brush away crumbs again after cutting cake.

Cutting cakes
For cleaner cutting lines and fewer crumbs, freeze the cake for 30 to 45 minutes.

When cutting each cake design, use the diagrams and photos as a guide and follow the directions carefully. A ruler and wooden picks are helpful to mark designs and act as a guide while cutting. The shaded areas

in the diagrams are unused portions of cake. Carefully position all pieces on a plate, tray or cake board. Connect the pieces with some of the frosting.

Leftover cake scraps can be used in a number of ways. Layer them with pudding or softened ice cream for a wonderful parfait. Serve under fresh berries and fruit as a sweet shortcake or use as the base for a trifle. Or, sprinkle crumbs on top of desserts or sundaes. And, easiest of all, they make a wonderful snack for hungry cooks and kids.

Assembling Cakes
Many decorated cakes are too large for standard plates and platters. Use cake boards,

cutting boards, cookie sheets or other large flat surfaces. Cake boards can be covered with foil, greaseproof paper, paper doilies or plastic wrap. To cover, cut the foil or paper 1 to 2 inches larger than the board. Center the board on the reverse side of the paper. Cut slashes in the paper almost to the board along any place that is curved. This allows the paper to fit smoothly over the board. Fold the edges over the board and tape into place. If a cake is very large or heavy, two cake boards may be stacked together before covering for additional support.

To keep the plate or covered board clean, tuck strips of waxed paper underneath the assembled cake before frosting. When decorating is complete, carefully slide out the strips and touch up frosting as needed.

THE FROSTING STORY
Frosting Consistency
The proper frosting consistency is the secret to successful decorating. Buttercream Frosting (page 95) should hold

its shape when scooped with a spatula. If the frosting is too soft because the kitchen is warm, try refrigerating the frosting for about 15 minutes and keep it chilled while you work. If the frosting is soft because liquid coloring was used or too much milk was added, beat in some additional sifted powdered sugar. If the frosting is too stiff to spread easily, beat in additional milk, a small amount at a time, until the desired consistency is achieved.

Canned Frostings
Commercially prepared canned frostings can also be used for cake decorating. Color and use for piping just like buttercream frosting. For best results, refrigerate the frosting first and keep chilled while decorating. One 16-ounce can of frosting equals about 1½ cups.

Base Frosting
Frosting cakes with Base Frosting (page 94) is a professional technique that is simple to do, gives the cake a smoother, cleaner finish and makes frosting the cake much easier. Spread a thin layer of

base frosting, or frosting thinned with milk, on all sides of the cake after cutting and positioning the pieces. This base coat helps to seal in the crumbs, preventing them from showing up in the final layer of buttercream frosting. Let the base frosting dry a few minutes before covering with buttercream frosting.

A glaze can be used instead of base frosting to add moistness, flavor and to seal in the crumbs. Brush the Jam Glaze (page 94) over the cut cake and allow it to set before frosting. Use a light-colored glaze for a cake with a white or light-colored frosting. A berry glaze is particularly good with a chocolate cake and chocolate frosting.

Coloring Frosting
We recommend you use paste colors (available at stores carrying cake decorating supplies) because they do not thin the frosting. If liquid food coloring is used, you may have to add more powdered sugar to get the frosting back to the desired consistency. When cocoa powder is added for flavor and color, some milk may need to be added.

To tint frosting with paste colors, add a small amount of the paste color with a wooden pick and stir well. Slowly add more color until the frosting is the desired shade. With liquid food colors, add the coloring drop by drop, mixing well after each drop, until the desired shade is reached. Paste colors are available in a wide variety of colors, but you can also make almost any color by mixing the basics: red, green, yellow, blue and black.

The following chart shows how these basic colors can be mixed to produce many frosting colors called for in this book. The numbers refer to the ratio of one color to another (i.e. orange is made by mixing 1 part red food coloring with 3 parts yellow food coloring). These ratios can be used for both paste and liquid food colorings.

To Make:	Red	Green	Yellow	Blue		Black
Rose	5			1	OR	1
Orange	1		3			
Peach	1		2			
Olive Green		2	1			1
Medium Blue				1		1
Purple	1			1		
Brown	2	2	1			

Storing Frosting

Buttercream frosting can be made ahead of time. Refrigerate it in an airtight container and use within two days. Or freeze it for up to one month. When ready to use, bring frosting to room temperature; beat well with electric mixer.

DECORATING TECHNIQUES

Frosting Cakes

To frost a cake, place a mound of frosting in the center of the cake. Spread frosting across the top by pushing it out toward the sides with a spatula. Always keep the spatula on a frosted surface, because once it touches the cake surface, crumbs will mix in with the frosting. To frost the sides, work from the top down, making sure the spatula only touches frosting.

Using a Pastry Bag

A coupler can save time and mess but it is not necessary for successful cake decorating. It is used to attach tips to the pastry bag and allows you to change tips without removing the frosting from the bag. To

use, unscrew the ring, insert the cone-shaped piece into the narrow end of the pastry bag until the end extends slightly beyond the end of the bag (snip off the end of the pastry bag if necessary), then place the decorating tip on the end. Screw the ring on to hold the tip in place. To change tips, unscrew the ring, remove the tip, place the new tip on and screw the ring back in place.

To fill a pastry bag with frosting, insert the decorating tip or attach the tip with a coupler. Fold the top of the bag down as shown, then use a spatula to place the frosting in the bag. Fill the bag only about half full, then unfold top of the bag. Twist top of the bag down tightly against the frosting.

Grip the pastry bag near top with the twisted end between thumb and forefinger. Place the other hand near the tip as shown. Using even pressure, squeeze the frosting out while guiding the tip. Do not loosen your grip on the twisted end or the frosting will begin to push up and out of the top of the bag.

Piped Decorations

Different decorating tips produce different piped decorations. Writing tips have round holes, and make smooth lines perfect for lettering and outlining. The basketweave tip can be used in two ways. The smooth side makes a wide flat ribbon of frosting. The ridged side makes a wide ridged

frosting stripe. A star tip makes individual stars or fancy ridged stripes and zigzags. With a little practice, there is no end to the variety of piped decorations you can make.

SERVING

Before serving cakes, remove any inedible decorations or wooden picks.

Portion size

The suggested number of servings for each cake is based on child-size portions served with ice cream. If several adults are included, the cake will serve fewer people.

HAVE FUN

Feel free to use your own colors and candies when decorating the cakes. Don't lock yourself in to the suggested decorations in the photos. You may want to match the cake to the party favors or use a child's favorite candies to decorate a cake. Try using one of the cake designs as the centerpiece for a birthday party and continue the theme of the cake with invitations, tablecloth, napkins and other decorations. Party games and take-home favors can also be coordinated to complete the theme. The important thing is to have fun and let your imagination and creativity take over.

TIPS FOR A SUCCESSFUL KID'S BIRTHDAY PARTY

Number of Guests

To determine the number of children to invite, take the age of the child, add one and invite that many guests. For example, a birthday party for a 5-year-old child might have a guest list of six children.

Party Themes

Choose a birthday cake and build a theme for the whole party around it. Add invitations, decorations and favors to match. Even the games can be related—pin the tail on the donkey can be changed to pin the tail on the dinosaur, or pin the nose on the teddy bear.

Invitations

Let the child be involved in all aspects of the party. He or she can help decide who to invite and make or choose the invitations. If you are making the invitations, choose the envelopes first and then design the card to fit. Be sure there is room for all pertinent information, including host or hostess of the party, date, time, place and R.S.V.P. information.

Party-Proofing Your Home

Decide what room(s) to use for the party. Remove anything that might get broken. Use festive plastic drop cloths or disposable table cloths to protect carpet and furniture. Plan activities that match the space available. If the room is small, choose games that can be played sitting down, like hot potato or telephone. During warmer months, outdoor games are great but be sure to have alternatives ready in case of rain.

Games and Activities

Most parties need not be longer than 2 hours to open presents, play games and have cake and ice cream. Keep the age of the children in mind when planning the games. They should challenge but not be too difficult to understand. A mixture of familiar games and a few new ones should keep the children busy and entertained. In order to keep everyone happy and avoid hurt feelings, try to plan non-competitive games or find alternative ways to play. Creative activities can be fun and they give each child a special gift to take home when the party is over. Whatever the activity—creating hats or masks, designing T-shirts or ornaments—start with something basic and let the children add decorations. Remember to protect the children's clothes and your furniture.

Party Favors

Everybody should leave the party with some little gift. The favors can be incorporated into the games (a treasure hunt) or passed out as the children leave. It is fun to match the favors to the theme—dinosaur erasers for a prehistoric party or a bandanna filled with treats for a train party.

Alphabet Block

CAKES & FROSTINGS
4 (8-inch) square cakes
1½ cups Base Frosting
(page 94), if desired
7 cups Buttercream
Frosting (page 95)*

DECORATIONS & EQUIPMENT
Pastel candy-coated
chocolate pieces
Chocolate sprinkles
Pink colored sugar
2 (19×13-inch) cake
boards**
Ice cream cone-shaped
cookie cutter
Pastry bag and medium
writing tip

1. Trim tops and edges of cakes to make tops level and all cakes of equal size.

2. Place 1 cake layer on covered cake board. Frost top with ¾ cup white frosting. Place second cake layer on frosting. Frost top with ¾ cup white frosting.

3. Place remaining cake board on top of cake. Top with third cake layer. Frost top with ¾ cup white frosting. Place fourth cake layer on top.

4. Frost entire cake with Base Frosting to seal in crumbs.

5. Frost opposite sides of cake with blue frosting. Frost remaining 2 sides with green frosting. Frost top of cake with 1 cup white frosting.

6. Outline edges with chocolate pieces as shown in photo.

7. Using cookie cutter, make outline on top of block. Using writing tip and remaining white frosting, pipe outline of design. Fill with sprinkles and colored sugar, as shown.

8. Slice and serve top 2 layers of cake first. To serve bottom section, remove cake board and slice into pieces.

Makes 32 to 36 servings

*Color 1½ cups frosting pastel blue and 1½ cups pastel green; reserve 4 cups white frosting.

**Cut one board into two 7×7-inch squares; stack and cover. Cut remaining board into 6½×6½-inch square.

BIRTHDAY WATCH

CAKES & FROSTINGS
  1 (8-inch) square cake
  1 (9-inch) round cake
  1 cup Base Frosting
    (page 94), if desired
  3½ cups Buttercream
    Frosting (page 95)*

DECORATIONS & EQUIPMENT
  Pink colored sugar
  Assorted candies
  1 (19×13-inch) cake
    board, cut to fit cake,
    if desired, and
    covered
  Pastry bag and medium
    writing tip

1. Trim tops and edges of cakes. Cut square cake as shown in diagram 1.

2. Position cakes on prepared cake board as shown in diagram 2, connecting with some of the medium pink frosting. Trim opposite ends to fit on cake board, if needed.

3. Frost entire cake with Base Frosting to seal in crumbs.

4. Frost top of round cake with light pink frosting, leaving 1-inch rim around edge. Frost sides and rim with blue frosting, reserving ½ cup for piping. Sprinkle blue area with colored sugar.

5. Frost band with medium pink frosting. Using writing tip and reserved blue frosting, pipe numbers and swirls on band as shown in photo. Arrange assorted candies on watch face.
    Makes 16 to 20 servings

Color 1½ cups frosting medium pink, 1 cup light pink and 1 cup blue.

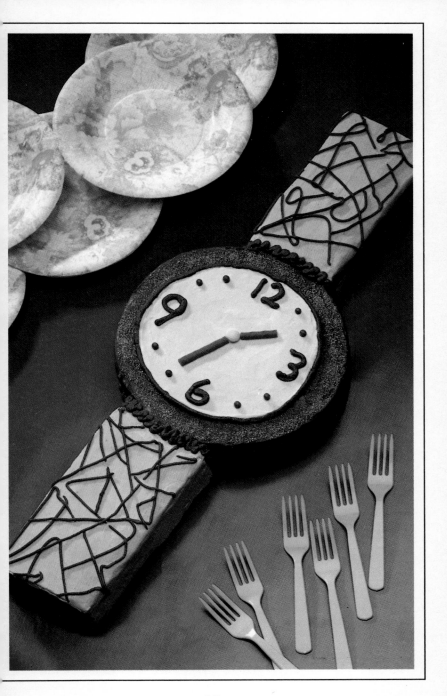

Boo the Ghost

CAKE & FROSTING
- 1 (13×9-inch) cake
- 2 cups Light & Fluffy Frosting (page 94)

DECORATIONS & EQUIPMENT
- 2 black licorice drops or jelly beans
- Plastic spiders, if desired
- 1 (19×13-inch) cake board, cut in half crosswise and covered

1. Trim top and edges of cake. Using diagram as guide, draw ghost pattern on 13×9-inch piece of waxed paper. Cut pattern out and place on cake. Cut out ghost. Place on prepared cake board.

2. Frost ghost, swirling frosting.

3. Arrange licorice drops for eyes and spiders as shown in photo.

Makes 12 to 14 servings

CATCH-U-LATER CALCULATOR

CAKE & FROSTINGS
    1 (13×9-inch) cake
    1 cup Base Frosting
        (page 94), if desired
    3 cups Buttercream
        Frosting (page 95)*

DECORATIONS & EQUIPMENT
    6 green candy discs
    10 pink candy discs
    1 (19×13-inch) cake
        board, cut in half
        crosswise and
        covered
        Pastry bag, medium and
        large writing tips

1. Trim top and edges of cake. Cut as shown in diagram 1.

2. Place piece B on prepared cake board. Attach piece A with some of the pink frosting, placing angled side toward opposite end of cake for calculator display area as shown in diagram 2.

3. Frost entire cake with Base Frosting to seal in crumbs.

4. Using wooden pick, draw area about 1 inch from edges of cake. Frost area with white frosting, as shown in photo.

5. Frost remaining cake with pink frosting.

6. Arrange candy discs as shown. Using medium writing tip and brown frosting, pipe numbers 0 through 9 on pink candy discs. Pipe decimal point, plus, minus, times, equal and division symbols on green candy discs.

7. Pipe a line around white area and pipe child's age in the display area. Using large writing tip, pipe border around display area.

Makes 16 to 20 servings

*Color 1½ cups frosting pink and ½ cup dark brown; reserve 1 cup white frosting.

COCOA THE CAT

CAKES & FROSTINGS
   1 (13×9-inch) cake
   1 (9-inch) round cake
   1½ cups Base Frosting
      (page 94), if desired
   2¾ cups Buttercream
      Frosting (page 95)*

DECORATIONS & EQUIPMENT
   1 cup flaked coconut,
      tinted brown**
   2½ cups flaked coconut,
      tinted tan**
   2 blue candies or
      gumballs
   1 black licorice whip
   1 small red gumdrop
   Assorted candies
   1 (19×13-inch) cake
      board, cut to fit cake,
      if desired, and
      covered
   Pastry bag and large
      writing tip

1. Trim tops and edges of cakes. Using diagram 1 as guide, draw cat body, ears and tail on 13×9-inch piece of waxed paper. Cut pattern out and place on cake. Cut out pieces. Cut one edge of round cake to form flat edge.

2. Position pieces on prepared cake board as shown in diagram 2, connecting with some of the cocoa frosting.

3. Frost entire cake with Base Frosting to seal in crumbs.

4. Frost again with cocoa frosting.

5. Using wooden pick, outline area for feet, tip of tail, edges of ears and face as shown in photo. Sprinkle with brown coconut.

6. Sprinkle remaining areas with tan coconut.

7. Using writing tip and blue frosting, pipe ovals for eyes; add blue candies.

8. Arrange short pieces of licorice whip for whiskers. Cut a slice off bottom of red gumdrop for nose. Arrange assorted candies for collar.
   Makes 18 to 22 servings

Mix 2½ cups frosting with 2 tablespoons unsweetened cocoa powder. Color ¼ cup frosting bright blue.

**See tip on tinting coconut, page 42.*

1

2

CORKY THE CLOWN

CAKES & FROSTINGS
1 (9-inch) square cake
1 (9-inch) round cake
1½ cups Base Frosting (page 94), if desired
3 cups Buttercream Frosting (page 95)*

DECORATIONS & EQUIPMENT
Assorted candies
1 (19×13-inch) cake board, cut to fit cake, if desired, and covered
Pastry bags, medium writing tip and star tip

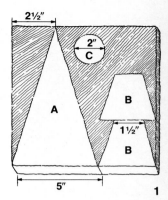

1. Trim tops and edges of cakes. Cut square cake as shown in diagram 1.

2. Position pieces on prepared cake board as shown in diagram 2, connecting with some of the white frosting.

3. Frost entire cake with Base Frosting to seal in crumbs.

4. Frost face with white frosting. Using writing tip and pink frosting, pipe mouth.

5. Frost bow tie and top of hat with yellow frosting as shown in photo. Frost hat with some of the orange frosting. Using star tip and orange frosting, pipe design on hat and bow tie.

6. Arrange assorted candies as shown.

Makes 16 to 18 servings

***Color ¾ cup frosting orange, ½ cup yellow and ¼ cup pink; reserve 1½ cups white frosting.**

DANCING FLOWER

CAKES & FROSTINGS
- 1 (8-inch) square cake
- 1 (9-inch) round cake
- 1½ cups Base Frosting (page 94), if desired
- 3 cups Buttercream Frosting (page 95)*

DECORATIONS & EQUIPMENT
- Thin chocolate wafer cookies
- Chocolate chips
- Assorted candies
- Spearmint candy leaves
- 1 (19×13-inch) cake board, covered
- Pastry bag and small writing tip

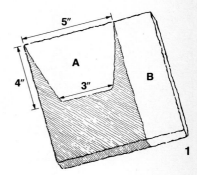

1. Trim tops and edges of cakes. Cut square cake as shown in diagram 1.

2. Position pieces on prepared cake board as shown in diagram 2, connecting with some of the pink frosting.

3. Frost entire cake with Base Frosting to seal in crumbs.

4. Frost as shown in photo. Arrange chocolate cookies around outer edge of round cake. Outline inside edge of circle with chocolate chips.

5. Using writing tip and blue frosting, pipe sunglasses as shown. Arrange candies for cheeks and mouth.

6. Add green leaves to stem; attach with frosting, if needed.
Makes 14 to 18 servings

Color 1½ cups frosting pink, ¾ cup yellow, ½ cup green and ¼ cup blue.

DREAM CASTLE

CAKES & FROSTINGS
- 3 (8-inch) square cakes
- 2 cups Base Frosting (page 94), if desired
- 5¼ cups Buttercream Frosting (page 95)*

DECORATIONS & EQUIPMENT
- Assorted colored sugar
- 4 sugar ice cream cones
- Small purple and white gumdrops
- Pastel candy-coated chocolate pieces
- 2 pink sugar wafer cookies
- 1 (19×13-inch) cake board, cut in half crosswise and covered

1. Trim tops and edges of cakes. Place one square cake on prepared cake board. Frost top with some of the white frosting.

2. Cut remaining cakes as shown in diagrams 1 and 2.

3. Place piece A over bottom layer. Frost top of piece A with some of the white frosting.

4. Position remaining pieces as shown in diagram 3, connecting with some of the white frosting.

5. Frost entire cake with Base Frosting to seal in crumbs.

6. Frost again with white frosting. Cover piece D (bridge) with colored sugar.

7. Frost cones with blue and yellow frostings. Place as shown in photo.

8. Decorate castle and towers as shown, using frosting to attach candies, if needed.

9. Arrange wafer cookies on front of castle for gate.

Makes 24 to 28 servings

Tip: *For easier frosting of cones, hold cone over fingers of one hand while frosting with other hand. Place in position, touching up frosting, if needed.*

Color ½ cup frosting blue and ½ cup yellow; reserve 4¼ cups white frosting.

1

2

3

27

FLYING KITES

CAKE & FROSTINGS
1 (13×9-inch) cake
1½ cups Base Frosting
(page 94), if desired
3½ cups Buttercream
Frosting (page 95)*

DECORATIONS & EQUIPMENT
4 small purple gumdrops
2 small green gumdrops
1 (19×13-inch) cake
board, covered
Pastry bags and
medium writing tip

1. Trim top and edges of cake. Cut as shown in diagram 1.

2. Position pieces on prepared cake board as shown in diagram 2 and photo, connecting with some of the frostings.

3. Frost cakes with Base Frosting to seal in crumbs.

4. Frost again as shown in photo, reserving small portion of each color frosting for piping.

5. Using writing tip, pipe reserved frostings onto kites in contrasting colors. Pipe crosspieces as shown from corner to corner, continuing onto board for tails.

6. Roll out gumdrops and cut each into a triangle.** Arrange triangles on tails of kites as shown.

Makes 16 to 20 servings

Color 1½ cups frosting rose, 1¼ cups light green and ¾ cup medium blue.

**To roll out gumdrops, place, small end up, on a surface lightly sprinkled with sugar. Roll to desired shape and thickness with rolling pin. Flattened gumdrops can be cut in the shape of flowers, leaves and other designs.*

28

Gingerbread Man

CAKE & FROSTINGS
1 (13×9-inch) cake
1 recipe Jam Glaze
   (page 94), if desired
2 cups Chocolate
   Buttercream Frosting
   (page 95)
½ cup Buttercream
   Frosting (page 95)

DECORATIONS & EQUIPMENT
Assorted candies
1 (19×13-inch) cake
   board, cut in half
   crosswise and
   covered
Pastry bag and medium
   writing tip

1. Trim top and edges of cake. Using diagram as guide, draw gingerbread man pattern on 13×9-inch piece of waxed paper. Cut pattern out and place on cake. Cut out gingerbread man. Place on prepared cake board.

2. Brush cake lightly with Jam Glaze. Let dry 1 hour.

3. Frost with chocolate frosting.

4. Using writing tip and white frosting, pipe as shown in photo.

5. Arrange assorted candies as shown.

Makes 10 to 14 servings

Bake a gingerbread man cookie for each child and leave it unfrosted. Provide colored frostings and assorted candies and let the children decorate their own cookies. If desired, before baking, make a hole in the top of each cookie. Thread ribbons through the holes of the baked cookies and decorate. The decorated cookies can then be used as Christmas ornaments.

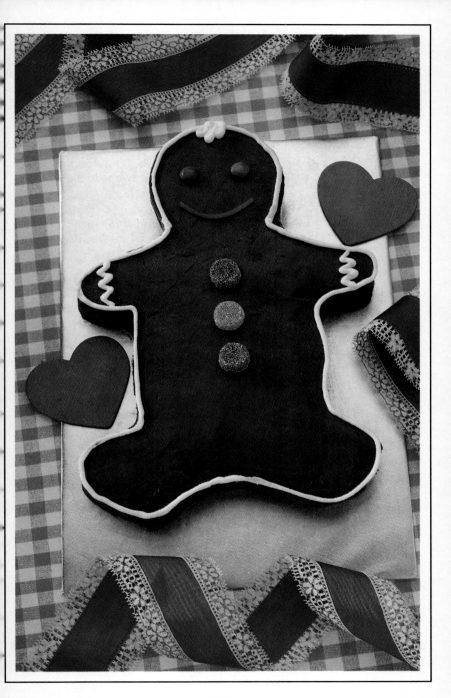

GUMBALL MACHINE

CAKES & FROSTINGS
1 (9-inch) round cake
1 (8-inch) square cake
1 cup Base Frosting
   (page 94), if desired
3½ cups Buttercream
   Frosting (page 95)*

DECORATIONS & EQUIPMENT
Gumballs
1 black licorice twist
   Foil-covered chocolate
   coins
1 red licorice whip
1 (19×13-inch) cake
   board, cut in half
   crosswise and
   covered

1. Trim tops and edges of cakes. Cut round cake as shown in diagram 1.

2. Position pieces on prepared cake board as shown in diagram 2, connecting with some of the white frosting.

3. Frost entire cake with Base Frosting to seal in crumbs.

4. Using wooden pick, draw coin insertion area as shown in photo. Frost with gray frosting. Frost remaining square cake with some of the red frosting.

5. Using wooden pick, draw area about 1 inch from top edge of round cake as shown. Frost area with red frosting.

6. Frost remaining round cake with white frosting and immediately decorate with gumballs.

7. Arrange pieces of black licorice around coin insertion area and place a foil-covered chocolate coin in center of area. Arrange red licorice as shown.

Makes 16 to 20 servings

Tip: *For younger children, use marshmallows or soft candies for gumballs.*

Color 1½ cups frosting red and ½ cup light gray; reserve 1½ cups white frosting.

7"

1

2

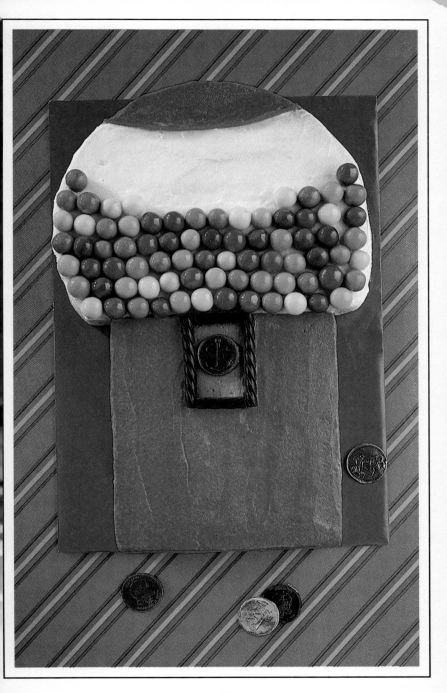

Happy Face

CAKE & FROSTINGS
- 1 (9-inch) round cake
- 1 cup Base Frosting (page 94), if desired
- 1¾ cups Buttercream Frosting (page 95)*

EQUIPMENT
- 1 (10-inch) round cake board, covered, or large plate
- Pastry bag and large writing tip

1. Trim top of cake. Place on prepared cake board.

2. Frost entire cake with Base Frosting to seal in crumbs.

3. Frost again with yellow frosting.

4. Using writing tip and cocoa frosting, pipe eyes and mouth as shown in photo.

Makes 10 to 12 servings

*Color 1½ cups frosting yellow. Mix ¼ cup frosting with 1 tablespoon unsweetened cocoa powder.

Variation: Can also be made as a 2 layer cake. Use two 9-inch round cakes and 3½ cups frosting; decorate as above.

Hot Air Balloon

CAKES & FROSTINGS
- **2 (9-inch) round cakes**
- **1½ cups Base Frosting (page 94), if desired**
- **3 cups Buttercream Frosting (page 95)***

DECORATIONS & EQUIPMENT
- **Candy-coated chocolate pieces**
- **Chocolate sprinkles**
- **2 black licorice twists**
- **Small plastic animals, if desired**
- **1 (19×13-inch) cake board, covered**

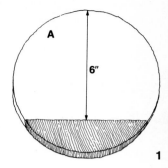

1. Trim tops of cakes. Cut cakes as shown in diagrams 1 and 2.

2. Position pieces on prepared cake board as shown in diagram 3, connecting with some of the yellow frosting.

3. Frost entire cake with Base Frosting to seal in crumbs.

4. Frost balloon as shown in photo. Decorate between colors with chocolate pieces.

5. Frost basket with cocoa frosting. Cover with chocolate sprinkles.

6. Arrange licorice twists for ropes.

7. Place plastic animals as passengers, if desired.

Makes 14 to 16 servings

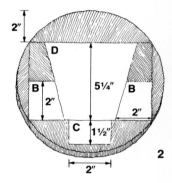

*Color 1¼ cups frosting yellow and ½ cup blue; reserve ½ cup white frosting. Mix remaining ¾ cup frosting with 1 tablespoon unsweetened cocoa powder.

JACK-O-LANTERN

CAKES & FROSTINGS
2 (10-inch) Bundt® cakes
2 cups Base Frosting
(page 94), if desired
5¼ cups Buttercream
Frosting (page 95)*

DECORATIONS & EQUIPMENT
Candy corn
2 (10-inch) round cake
boards, stacked and
covered, or large plate
1 (6-ounce) paper cup or
ice cream wafer cone
Pastry bag and medium
writing tip

1. Trim flat sides of cakes.
Place one cake on prepared
cake board, flat-side up.

2. Frost top of cake with some
of the orange frosting. Place
second cake, flat-side down,
over frosting.

3. Frost entire cake with Base
Frosting to seal in crumbs.

4. Frost again with orange
frosting.

5. Hold cup over fingers of one
hand. Using other hand, frost
cup with green frosting. Place
upside-down in center of cake
to form stem. Touch up frosting,
if needed.

6. Using writing tip and brown
frosting, pipe eyes and mouth.
Arrange candy corn for teeth as
shown in photo.

7. Before serving, remove stem.
Slice and serve top cake first,
then bottom.

Makes 36 to 40 servings

*Color 4½ cups frosting
orange, ½ cup dark green and
¼ cup dark brown.*

Dressing up is always fun at
parties. So for a creative
activity, provide plain masks
or hats to be decorated by
each child. Have lots of
paints, markers, construction
paper, crepe paper, yarn and
glitter available. Stickers are
also an easy way to
decorate. Awards can be
given for the scariest or most
creative—just be sure every
child wins something.

JET PLANE

CAKE & FROSTINGS
1 (13×9-inch) cake
1 cup Base Frosting
(page 94), if desired
3½ cups Buttercream
Frosting (page 95)*

DECORATIONS & EQUIPMENT
4 pastel miniature
marshmallows
1 small red gumdrop
1 (19×13-inch) cake
board, cut to fit cake,
if desired, and
covered
Pastry bag and medium
writing tip

1. Trim top and edges of cake. Cut as shown in diagram 1.

2. Place piece A in center of prepared cake board. Frost top with some of the white frosting, then place piece B over frosting. Starting 3 inches from 1 side make an angled cut in piece B toward the front as shown in diagram 2.

3. Position remaining pieces on prepared cake board as shown in diagram 3, connecting with some of the white frosting. Trim sides to make nose about 1 inch wide. Trim top side edges of piece B to give a rounded appearance as shown in photo.

4. Frost entire cake with Base Frosting to seal in crumbs.

5. Using wooden pick, draw areas for windows as shown. Frost with light gray frosting.

6. Frost remaining cake with white frosting.

7. Using writing tip and blue frosting, pipe outlines for windows and design on wings as shown. Attach flattened marshmallows and gumdrop as shown.

Makes 14 to 16 servings

Color ½ cup frosting blue and ½ cup light gray; reserve 2½ cups white frosting.

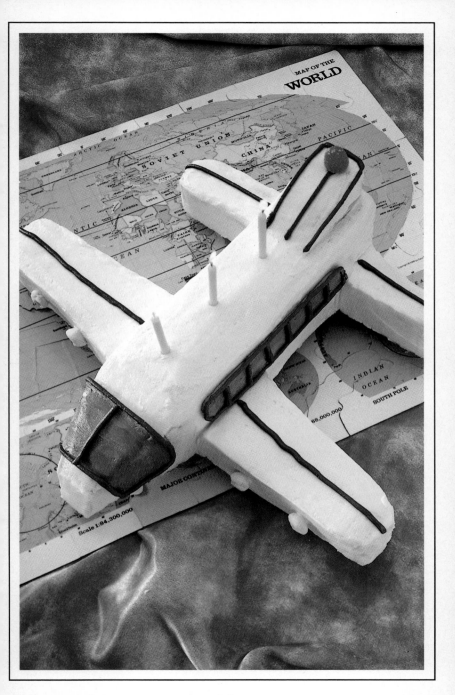

Legs the Caterpillar

CAKES & FROSTING
- 6 medium (2¾-inch) cupcakes
- 1 jumbo (4-inch) cupcake
- 3½ cups Buttercream Frosting (page 95), colored yellow

DECORATIONS & EQUIPMENT
- 2 cups flaked coconut, tinted yellow to match frosting*
- 6 purple gumdrops
- 2 small purple candies or gumballs
- 2 small black licorice drops
- 1 black licorice whip
- Red licorice whips
- 1 (19×13-inch) cake board, cut in half lengthwise and covered

1. Frost sides and bottoms of medium cupcakes and roll in coconut, one at a time. Arrange, unfrosted-side down, in zigzag line on prepared cake board as shown in photo. Place gumdrops in center of each cupcake.

2. Frost side and bottom of jumbo cupcake. Roll in coconut, leaving one side plain for face. Place at front of cupcake line.

3. Arrange candies on large cupcake for face. Insert short pieces of the black licorice whip into center of licorice drops for antennas; place as shown. Cut red licorice whips into small pieces and arrange as legs.

Makes 7 servings

*To tint coconut, combine small amount of food coloring (paste or liquid) with 1 teaspoon water in large bowl. Add coconut and stir until evenly coated. Add more coloring, if needed.

Variation: More cupcakes can be added to serve more children. Add about ⅓ cup frosting and about ¼ cup flaked coconut for each additional cupcake.

LET'S PLAY BALL!

CAKES & FROSTINGS
   1½ cups cake batter
   1 (9-inch) round cake
   1 recipe Jam Glaze
      (page 94), if desired
   1½ cups Chocolate
      Buttercream Frosting
      (page 95)
   2 cups Buttercream
      Frosting (page 95)*

DECORATIONS & EQUIPMENT
   1 black licorice whip
   1 (10-inch) round cake
      board, covered, or
      large plate
   Pastry bags, small and
      medium writing tips

1. Preheat oven to 350°F. Grease and flour 1-quart ovenproof bowl. Pour 1½ cups cake batter into prepared bowl. Bake 40 minutes or until wooden skewer inserted into center comes out clean. Let cool in bowl 10 minutes. Loosen edge; invert on wire rack and cool completely.

2. Trim top of round cake and flat side of bowl cake. Cut round cake as shown in diagram; place on prepared cake board.

3. Brush cake lightly with Jam Glaze. Let dry 1 hour.

4. Frost glove with chocolate frosting. Using medium writing tip and black frosting, pipe around edge of glove, forming fingers of glove as shown in photo.

5. Cut licorice whip into four 2-inch pieces. Crisscross across space between thumb and fingers of glove.

6. Place bowl cake on glove flat-side down. Frost with white frosting.

7. Using small writing tip and red frosting, pipe seams on baseball as shown.

44

8. Serve baseball first, then glove.

Makes 16 to 18 servings

*Color ½ cup frosting black and ½ cup red; reserve 1 cup white frosting.

Lucy the Ladybug

CAKE & FROSTINGS
   4 cups of cake batter
   1¾ cups Buttercream
      Frosting (page 95)*

DECORATIONS & EQUIPMENT
   Assorted candies
   1 (10-inch) round cake
      board, covered, or
      large plate
   Pastry bag and medium
      writing tip

1. Preheat oven to 350°F. Grease and flour 2-quart ovenproof bowl. Pour 4 cups of cake batter into prepared bowl. Bake 1 hour and 15 minutes or until wooden skewer inserted into center comes out clean. Cool 15 minutes in bowl. Loosen edge; invert on wire rack and cool completely.

2. Trim flat side of cake. Place on prepared cake board, flat-side down.

3. Using wooden pick, mark a semicircle about 3 inches from edge of cake for head as shown in photo.

4. Frost remainder of cake with red frosting. Frost head with cocoa frosting, reserving small portion for piping.

5. Using writing tip and reserved cocoa frosting, pipe line down center from head to other edge. Pipe line between head and body.

6. Arrange assorted candies as shown.

Makes 14 to 18 servings

*Color 1 cup frosting red. Mix ¾ cup frosting with 2 tablespoons unsweetened cocoa powder and 2 teaspoons milk.

A summer birthday is the perfect opportunity for an outdoor party. Plan games that take advantage of the extra space outdoors, such as races or tug of war. Or include a trip to a baseball game or the beach. Playing outside leads to hearty appetites so have substantial food prepared. Hot dogs and hamburgers with all the fixings are ideal.

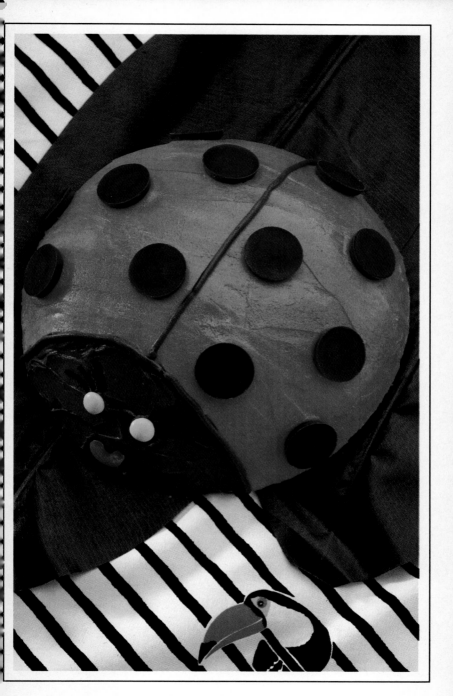

Ninja Turtle

CAKE & FROSTINGS
1 (9-inch) round cake
1 cup Base Frosting
(page 94), if desired
2¾ cups Buttercream
Frosting (page 95)*

DECORATIONS & EQUIPMENT
2 black jelly beans
Blue ribbon
1 (10-inch) round cake
board, covered, or
large plate
Pastry bags and
medium writing tip

1. Place knife on cake edge, ¾ inch down. Make wedge cut (piece A) by moving the knife up and toward the center as shown in diagram 1. Attach piece A to uncut side with some of the green frosting, placing thin edge near the center as shown in diagram 2.

2. Place cake on prepared cake board. Frost entire cake with Base Frosting to seal in crumbs.

3. Using wooden pick, draw mask as shown in photo, continuing down sides of cake. Frost with blue frosting. Frost remainder of cake with green frosting, mounding nose area.

4. Using writing tip and dark gray frosting, pipe mouth. Use spoon to add red frosting as shown.

5. Pipe light gray frosting into ovals for eyes. Add jelly beans.

6. Attach small pieces of blue ribbon to side of cake for ends of mask.

Makes 10 to 12 servings

Color 1½ cups frosting green, ½ cup blue, ¼ cup dark gray, ¼ cup light gray and 1 tablespoon red.

Variation: Can be made as a 2-layer cake. Use 2 (9-inch) round cakes and increase green frosting to 2½ cups; decorate as above.

P.C. THE COMPUTER

CAKES & FROSTINGS
    1 (9-inch) square cake
    1 (13×9-inch) cake
  1½ cups Base Frosting
      (page 94), if desired
    3 cups Buttercream
      Frosting (page 95)*

DECORATIONS & EQUIPMENT
  Blue colored sugar
  Pastel candy-coated
    chocolate pieces
  1 pink sugar wafer cookie
  1 (19×13-inch) cake
    board, cut in half
    crosswise and
    covered
  Pastry bag and medium
    writing tip

1. Trim tops and edges of cakes. Cut 2 inches from one side of square cake. Place on prepared cake board.

2. Cut 13×9-inch cake in half crosswise. Frost top of 1 half with some of the blue frosting. Place remaining half on frosting. Position upright against square cake as shown in diagram, connecting with some of the blue frosting. Insert wooden picks or small wooden skewers for additional support, if needed.

3. Frost entire cake with Base Frosting to seal in crumbs.

4. Using wooden pick, draw area for screen, about 1½ inches from edges, as shown in photo. Frost screen with gray frosting.

5. Frost remaining cake with blue frosting. Sprinkle top of cake with colored sugar. Arrange rows of chocolate pieces and wafer cookie for keyboard.

6. Using writing tip and pink frosting, pipe an outline around gray area and "Happy Birthday" on screen.

7. To serve, remove wooden picks. Lay upright part of cake flat before cutting.
Makes 28 to 32 servings

Color 2 cups frosting blue, ½ cup light gray and ½ cup pink.

PICK-UP TRUCK

CAKE & FROSTINGS
    1 (13×9-inch) cake
    1 cup Base Frosting
        (page 94), if desired
    2½ cups Buttercream
        Frosting (page 95)*

DECORATIONS & EQUIPMENT
    1 black licorice whip
    4 chocolate sandwich
        cookies
    4 large nonpareils
        Jelly beans
    1 (19×13-inch) cake
        board, cut in half
        lengthwise or to fit
        cake, if desired, and
        covered
    Pastry bag and medium
        writing tip

1. Trim top and edges of cake. Cut as shown in diagram 1. Place piece A on prepared cake board. Frost top of piece A with some of the yellow frosting.

2. Place piece B on piece A about 3½ inches in from short end as shown in diagram 2. Position remaining pieces on piece A as shown in diagram 2, connecting with some of the yellow frosting.

3. Frost entire cake with Base Frosting to seal in crumbs.

4. Frost 3 sides of piece B with white frosting for windows.

5. Frost remainder of cake with yellow frosting, reserving small portion for piping.

6. Using writing tip and reserved yellow frosting, pipe border around windows as shown in photo. Cut licorice whip into pieces and place on windshield for wipers. Position cookies for wheels. Attach nonpareils for lights and place jelly beans in bed of truck.

Makes 10 to 14 servings

*Color 2 cups frosting yellow; reserve ½ cup white frosting.

Practically Pizza

CAKE & FROSTINGS
1 (9-inch) round cake
1 cup Base Frosting (page 94), if desired
1¾ cups Buttercream Frosting (page 95)*
1¼ cups Uncooked Fondant (page 94)**

EQUIPMENT
1 (10-inch) round cake board, covered, or small pizza pan or wooden board
Pastry bag and extra large writing tip

1. Trim top of cake. Place cake on prepared cake board.

2. Frost entire cake with Base Frosting to seal in crumbs.

3. Frost side of cake and 1-inch rim with some of the cocoa frosting.

4. Frost remainder of cake with red frosting.

5. Using writing tip and remaining cocoa frosting, pipe around rim for raised crust. Flatten slightly with back of spoon.

6. For olives, roll green fondant to rectangle about ¾ inch wide and ¼ inch thick. Form red fondant into log about ¼ inch in diameter. Place red fondant on one long edge of green fondant; roll up jelly-roll style. Seal edges. Refrigerate until firm. Cut crosswise into thin slices and flatten slightly.

7. For pepperoni, knead reddish-brown fondant and 1 tablespoon white fondant together lightly (some white should still be visible). Form into roll about 1 inch in diameter. Refrigerate until firm. Cut crosswise into thin slices.

8. For cheese, shape remaining white fondant into log, about 1½ inches in diameter. Refrigerate until very firm. Using cheese shredder, shred fondant over pizza.

9. Arrange olives and pepperoni on pizza.

Makes 10 to 12 servings

Tip: *Use rolled green and white gumdrops (see page 28) cut into small pieces for chopped bell pepper and onion.*

*Color 1 cup frosting red. Mix ¾ cup frosting with 2 teaspoons unsweetened cocoa powder.

**Color 3 tablespoons fondant olive green, 3 tablespoons reddish-brown and 1 tablespoon red; reserve ¾ cup white fondant.

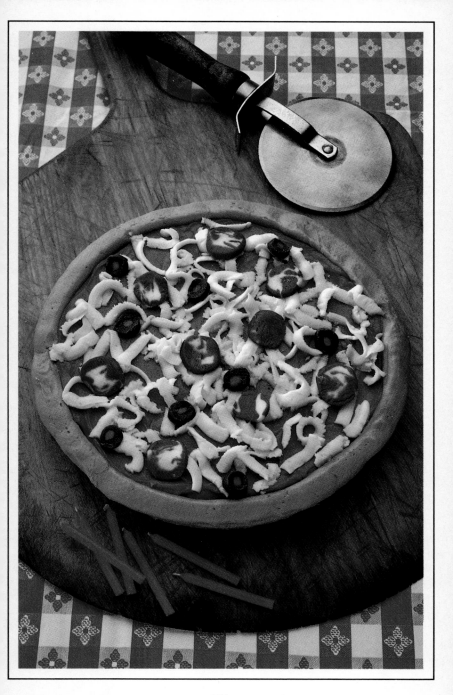

55

Princess Doll

CAKES & FROSTINGS
4 cups cake batter
1 (8-inch) round cake
1 cup Base Frosting
(page 94), if desired
3 cups Buttercream
Frosting (page 95),
colored peach

DECORATIONS & EQUIPMENT
Pastel miniature
marshmallows
Small chocolate
nonpareils
1 (10-inch) round cake
board, covered, or
large plate
1 doll body and head*

1. Preheat oven to 350°F. Grease and flour 2-quart ovenproof bowl. Pour 4 cups cake batter into prepared bowl. Bake 1 hour and 15 minutes or until wooden skewer inserted into center comes out clean. Cool 15 minutes in bowl. Loosen edge; invert on wire rack and cool completely.

2. Trim flat side of bowl cake and top of round cake. Trim round cake even with bowl cake. Place round cake on prepared cake board. Frost top with some of the peach frosting. Place bowl cake, flat-side down, on frosting.

3. Frost entire cake with Base Frosting to seal in crumbs.

4. Make small V-shaped hole in center of cake; insert doll in hole. (To keep doll's clothing clean, wrap bottom of doll in plastic wrap.)

5. Frost cake with peach frosting. Decorate skirt with flattened marshmallows as shown in photo. Decorate bottom of skirt with chocolate nonpareils.

6. To serve, remove doll and slice cake into small wedges.
Makes 14 to 18 servings

Doll body and head can be purchased from stores carrying cake decorating supplies. If desired, use doll with legs removed or covered in plastic wrap.

Radio Fun

CAKE & FROSTINGS
- 1 (9-inch) square cake
- 1 cup Base Frosting (page 94), if desired
- 3 cups Buttercream Frosting (page 95)*

DECORATIONS & EQUIPMENT
- Pink and black licorice pieces
- 2 yellow candy discs
- 1 orange flat gumdrop
- 1 (19×13-inch) cake board, cut into 10×10-inch square and covered
- Icing comb
- Pastry bags, small writing tip and basketweave tip

1. Trim top and edges of cake. Cut as shown in diagram.

2. Place cake on prepared cake board.

3. Frost entire cake with Base Frosting to seal in crumbs.

4. Frost as shown in photo, reserving small portion of each color for piping. While frosting is soft, use icing comb as shown in photo below to make design for speaker.**

5. Using flat side of basketweave tip and reserved yellow frosting, pipe two vertical lines, one at end of speaker section and another 2 inches from the first line.

6. Using writing tip and reserved green frosting, pipe accents on handle as shown.

7. Position candies as shown.
Makes 10 to 14 servings

Color 2 cups frosting green and 1 cup yellow.

Design on speaker can also be made with fork.

Rex the Dinosaur ▮▮

CAKE & FROSTINGS
1 (13×9-inch) cake
2 cups Buttercream
Frosting (page 95),
colored green
1 recipe Jam Glaze
(page 94)

DECORATIONS & EQUIPMENT
Assorted candies
1 (19×13-inch) cake
board, cut to fit cake,
if desired, and
covered

1. Trim top and edges of cake. Using diagram 1 as guide, draw pattern pieces on 13×9-inch piece of waxed paper. Cut pattern out and place on cake. Cut out dinosaur pieces.

2. Position pieces on prepared cake board as shown in diagram 2, connecting with some of the green frosting.

3. Brush cake lightly with Jam Glaze. Let dry about 1 hour.

4. Frost cake with green frosting.

5. Decorate with assorted candies as shown in photo.
Makes 8 to 10 servings

1

B

A

C

2

61

CAKES & FROSTINGS
1 (9-inch) round cake
1 (8-inch) square cake
**1 cup Base Frosting
    (page 94), if desired**
**3½ cups Buttercream
    Frosting (page 95)***

DECORATIONS & EQUIPMENT
**Assorted candies or
    gumballs**
**Pink and white sugar
    wafer cookies**
**1 (19×13-inch) cake
    board, cut in half
    crosswise and
    covered**
**Pastry bags and
    basketweave tip**

1. Trim tops and edges of cakes. Cut round cake as shown in diagram 1.

2. Position pieces on prepared cake board as shown in diagram 2, connecting with some of the blue frosting. Trim sides of round cake to match sides of square cake, if necessary.

3. Frost entire cake with Base Frosting to seal in crumbs.

4. Using wooden pick, draw line across cake 1 inch up from bottom. Frost area with some of the white frosting as shown in photo. Frost remaining square cake with some of the blue frosting.

5. Draw line 4 inches above frosted blue area. Frost area with gray frosting.

6. Divide remaining area in half vertically; frost areas with blue and white frosting as shown, reserving small portion of each color for piping.

7. Using flat side of basketweave tip and reserved white frosting, pipe vertical line dividing white and blue frosting.

8. Using flat side of basketweave tip and reserved blue frosting, pipe border between blue and gray frosting as shown.

9. Decorate with assorted candies and wafer cookies as shown.

Makes 16 to 20 servings

***Color 1½ cups frosting blue
and 1 cup gray; reserve 1 cup
white frosting.***

63

Sailboat

CAKE & FROSTINGS

1 (13×9-inch) cake
1 cup Base Frosting
   (page 94), if desired
3½ cups Buttercream
   Frosting (page 95)*

DECORATIONS & EQUIPMENT

5 white licorice drops or
   gumballs
1 black licorice twist
1 black licorice whip
   Small flag, if desired
1 (19×13-inch) cake
   board, cut to fit cake,
   if desired, and
   covered

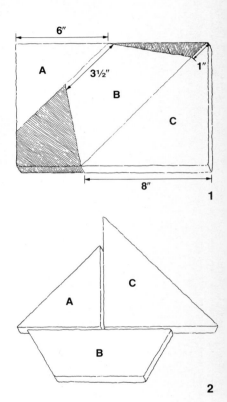

1. Trim top and edges of cake. Cut as shown in diagram 1.

2. Position pieces on prepared cake board as shown in diagram 2, connecting with some of the green frosting.

3. Frost entire cake with Base Frosting to seal in crumbs.

4. Frost again as shown in photo.

5. Arrange candies as shown. Place flag on top.

Makes 12 to 14 servings

Color 1½ cups frosting green and 1¼ cups peach; reserve ¾ cup white frosting.

Skateboard

CAKES & FROSTINGS
1 (9-inch) round cake
1 (13×9-inch) cake
**1½ cups Base Frosting
(page 94), if desired**
**3½ cups Buttercream
Frosting (page 95)***

DECORATIONS & EQUIPMENT
5 green jelly beans
5 purple jelly beans
**8 chocolate sandwich
cookies**
**1 (19×13-inch) cake
board**
**Foot-shaped cookie
cutter**
**Pastry bags, medium
writing tip and
basketweave tip**

1. Trim tops and edges of cakes. Cut round cake in half crosswise. Frost top of one half with some of the orange frosting. Place remaining half on frosting. Starting from round side, near top of cake, make an angled cut almost to bottom layer to form wedge as shown in diagram 1.

2. Cut cakes as shown in diagram 2.

3. Using diagram 2 as a guide, draw shape of cake on cake board. Cut cake board slightly smaller and cover.

4. Place cakes on prepared cake board as shown in diagram 3, connecting with some of the orange frosting.

5. Frost entire cake with Base Frosting to seal in crumbs.

6. Frost again with orange frosting. Using cookie cutter or wooden pick, draw outlines of feet as shown in photo. Using writing tip and green and purple frostings, pipe around outlines of feet. Place jelly beans on feet for toes.

7. Using plain side of basketweave tip, pipe white frosting as shown.

8. Connect cookies in pairs with white frosting to make 4 sets of wheels. Lay each pair flat on cutting board and cut small amount off tops and bottoms of cookies to form flat edges.

9. Use frosting to attach wheels to underside of cake board.
Makes 20 to 24 servings

Tip: Set skateboard on tray when moving. For easier serving, remove wheels before cutting.

*Color 2½ cups frosting orange, ¼ cup green and ¼ cup purple; reserve ½ cup white frosting.

1

7″

3½″

2

3

Snowy the Snowman

CAKES & FROSTINGS

- 2 (9-inch) round cakes*
- 1 medium cupcake
- 1½ cups Base Frosting (page 94), if desired
- 3½ cups Buttercream Frosting (page 95)**

DECORATIONS & EQUIPMENT

- 3 cups flaked coconut
- 2 large black gumdrops
- Assorted candies
- 2 (10-inch) round cake boards, taped together and covered, or large tray

1. Trim tops of cakes. Cut as shown in diagrams 1 and 2.

2. Position pieces on prepared cake board as shown in diagram 3, connecting with some of the white frosting.

3. Frost entire cake with Base Frosting to seal in crumbs.

4. Frost again with white frosting. Cover with coconut. Frost hat with gray frosting.

5. Cut a thin slice off each black gumdrop; use for eyes. Arrange assorted candies as shown in photo.

Makes 14 to 16 servings

*Before baking round cakes, reserve enough batter for 1 cupcake.

**Color ½ cup frosting dark gray or black; reserve 3 cups white frosting.

68

Soccer Ball

CAKE & FROSTINGS
  4 cups cake batter
  1 cup Base Frosting
    (page 94), if desired
  2½ cups Buttercream
    Frosting (page 95)

DECORATIONS & EQUIPMENT
  Red licorice whips
  Red colored sugar
  1 (10-inch) round cake
    board, covered, or
    large plate

1. Preheat oven to 350°F. Grease and flour 3-quart ovenproof bowl. Pour cake batter into prepared bowl. Bake 1 hour and 15 minutes or until wooden skewer inserted into center comes out clean. Cool 15 minutes in bowl. Loosen edge; invert on wire rack and cool completely.

2. Trim flat side of cake. Place on prepared cake board. Trim edges into ball shape.

3. Frost entire cake with Base Frosting to seal in crumbs. Frost again with white frosting.

4. Using wooden pick, draw a pentagon (with five 1½-inch sides) in center of top of cake. Surround pentagon with five hexagons (each with six 1½-inch sides). Repeat pattern alternating pentagons and hexagons to cover entire ball as shown in diagram.

5. Cut licorice whips into 1½-inch pieces. Outline shapes with licorice. Fill pentagon shapes with colored sugar.
  Makes 14 to 16 servings

Variation: *Color 1 cup of frosting bright blue. Using extra large writing tip and blue frosting, pipe frosting inside pentagon shapes, then smooth with small spatula.*

CAKES & FROSTINGS

1 (13×9-inch) cake
1 (9-inch) square cake
1½ cups Base Frosting
    (page 94), if desired
3 cups Buttercream
    Frosting (page 95)*

EQUIPMENT

1 (19×13-inch) cake
    board, cut to fit cake,
    if desired, and
    covered
    Pastry bag and medium
    writing tip

1. Trim tops and edges of cakes. Cut 13×9-inch cake as shown in diagram 1. Cut square cake as shown in diagram 2.

2. Place piece A in center of prepared cake board. Frost top with some of the white frosting. Place piece B over frosting as shown in diagram 3.

3. Starting 3½ inches from 1 side make an angled cut toward front to form nose, cutting through top and some of bottom layer as shown in diagram 3.

4. Position remaining pieces on prepared cake board as shown in diagram 4, connecting with some of the white frosting. Trim sides to make nose about 1 inch wide.

5. Frost entire cake with Base Frosting to seal in crumbs.

6. Using wooden pick, draw areas for window and nose as shown in photo. Frost window with light gray frosting. Frost nose with dark gray frosting, reserving small portion for piping.

7. Frost remaining areas with white frosting.

8. Using writing tip and reserved dark gray frosting, pipe stripes on wings and tail and outline window as shown. Pipe "USA" on wings.

Makes 14 to 16 servings

*Color ¼ cup frosting light gray and ¼ cup dark gray or black; reserve 2½ cups white frosting.

3

4

73

SPEEDY RACETRACK

CAKES & FROSTINGS
   1 (9-inch) round cake
   1 (13×9-inch) cake
   1½ cups Base Frosting
      (page 94), if desired
   3½ cups Buttercream
      Frosting (page 95)*

DECORATIONS & EQUIPMENT
   Green colored sugar
   2 to 3 rolls white donut-
      shaped hard candies,
      cut in half
   ½ (16-ounce) box
      cinnamon graham
      crackers
   2- to 3-inch race cars
   Flags, if desired
   1 (19×13-inch) cake
      board, cut to fit cake,
      if desired, and
      covered

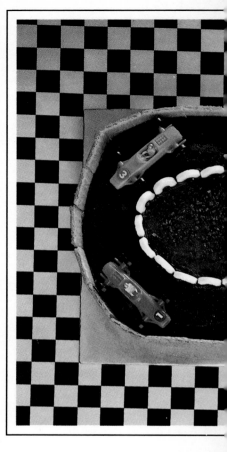

1. Trim tops and edges of cakes. Cut round cake in half crosswise. Cut 13×9-inch cake as shown in diagram 1.

2. Position pieces on prepared cake board as shown in diagram 2, connecting with some of the green frosting.

3. Frost entire cake with Base Frosting to seal in crumbs.

4. Using wooden pick, draw area for track, about 2 inches wide, as shown in photo. Frost center of cake with green frosting. Sprinkle with colored sugar. Frost track and sides of cake with gray frosting.

5. Arrange hard candies, cut-side down, around inside of track. Cut graham crackers about ¼ inch higher than cake. Arrange around edge of cake, attaching with more gray frosting, if needed.

6. Let frosting harden before placing cars and flags on track.
      Makes 20 to 24 servings

*Color 2 cups dark gray or blue and 1½ cups green.

1"

1

2

STRAWBERRY ICE CREAM CONE

CAKES & FROSTINGS
    1 (9-inch) round cake
    1 (13×9-inch) cake
    2 cups Base Frosting
        (page 94), if desired
    3½ cups Buttercream
        Frosting (page 95)*

DECORATIONS & EQUIPMENT
    Red gumdrops, cut in
        small pieces
    1 (19×13-inch) cake
        board, cut to fit cake,
        if desired, and
        covered
    Pastry bag and
        basketweave tip

1. Trim tops and edges of cakes. Cut cakes as shown in diagram 1.

2. Position pieces on prepared cake board as shown in diagram 2, connecting with some of the pink frosting.

3. Frost entire cake with Base Frosting to seal in crumbs.

4. Frost round cake with pink frosting. Arrange small pieces of gumdrops in frosting.

5. Frost cone with cocoa frosting, reserving ½ cup. Using basketweave tip and reserved frosting, pipe as shown in photo.

       Makes 18 to 22 servings

Mix 2 cups frosting with ¼ cup unsweetened cocoa powder; color 1½ cups frosting pink.

TEDDY BEAR TRAIN

CAKE & FROSTINGS

1 (13×9-inch) cake
3 cups Base Frosting
(page 94), if desired
6 cups Buttercream
Frosting (page 95)*

DECORATIONS & EQUIPMENT

1 large marshmallow
1 round chocolate candy
Teddy bear cookies or
animal crackers
Assorted candies and
cookies
32 chocolate discs
Flat wooden craft sticks
1 (19×13-inch) cake
board, cut in half
lengthwise, short
ends taped together,
and covered
Non-toxic glue

1. Arrange wooden sticks equal distance apart on covered cake board. Glue in place.

2. Trim top and edges of cake.

3. Cut cake as shown in diagram 1.

4. Place piece A on top of 1 of the other pieces, connecting with some of the red frosting as shown in diagram 2.

5. Frost sides and tops of pieces with Base Frosting to seal in crumbs.

6. Frost engine with red frosting. Place large marshmallow on engine and top with chocolate candy as shown in photo.

7. Frost remaining pieces with each of the different colors. Press cookies onto sides.

8. Using spatula, carefully place cars on track, starting with the engine and spacing evenly apart. Arrange assorted candies and cookies on top of each car. Arrange 4 chocolate discs, 2 per side, on each car for wheels as shown.

Makes 14 to 16 servings

*Color ¾ cup frosting __each__ red, medium blue, yellow, orange, green, pink, purple and dark blue.

1

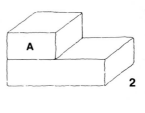

2

79

Telly Phone

CAKE & FROSTINGS
1 (13×9-inch) cake
1 cup Base Frosting
(page 94), if desired
2 cups Buttercream
Frosting (page 95)*

DECORATIONS & EQUIPMENT
Pink colored sugar
Assorted candies
1 (19×13-inch) cake
board, cut in half
crosswise and
covered
Pastry bag and small
writing tip

1. Trim top and edges of cake. Cut as shown in diagram.

2. Position pieces on prepared cake board as shown in photo.

3. Frost entire cake with Base Frosting to seal in crumbs.

4. Using wooden pick, draw 5-inch circle for dial area as shown in photo. Frost area with white frosting, reserving small portion for piping.

5. Frost remaining cake with purple frosting; sprinkle with colored sugar.

6. Using writing tip and reserved frosting, pipe line around dial as shown.

7. Decorate cake with assorted candies as shown.
Makes 10 to 14 servings

*Color 1½ cups frosting purple; reserve ½ cup white frosting.

Tic-Tac-Toe

CAKE & FROSTINGS
- 1 (8-inch) square cake
- 1 cup Base Frosting (page 94), if desired
- 1½ cups Buttercream Frosting (page 95)

DECORATIONS & EQUIPMENT
- 4 black licorice twists
- 3 large red gumdrops
- 24 small red candies
- 1 (19×13-inch) cake board, cut in half crosswise and covered, or large plate

1. Trim top and edges of cake. Place on prepared cake board.

2. Frost entire cake with Base Frosting to seal in crumbs.

3. Frost again with buttercream frosting.

4. Using wooden pick, mark cake into thirds, both horizontally and vertically. Arrange 2 licorice twists over horizontal lines; cut and place remaining licorice twists as shown in photo.

5. Decorate with gumdrops and candies as shown.

Makes 9 to 12 servings

TOUCHDOWN FOOTBALL

CAKE & FROSTINGS
1 (13×9-inch) cake
1 recipe Jam Glaze
(page 94), if desired
3½ cups Chocolate
Buttercream Frosting
(page 95)

DECORATIONS & EQUIPMENT
Black licorice whips
Red candy-coated
chocolate pieces
Purchased "Happy
Birthday" decoration
1 (10-inch) round cake
board, cut to fit cake,
if desired, and covered,
or large plate

1. Trim top and edges of cake.
Cut cake in half crosswise.
Frost top of one half with some
of the chocolate frosting. Place
remaining half on frosting.

2. Cut football shape as shown
in diagram. Brush cake lightly
with Jam Glaze. Let dry 1 hour.

3. Frost with chocolate frosting,
mounding frosting slightly
on top.

4. Decorate as shown in photo,
using licorice for laces.
Makes 10 to 14 servings

T-RIFFIC BIRTHDAY T-SHIRT

CAKE & FROSTINGS
   1 (13×9-inch) cake
   1 cup Base Frosting
      (page 94), if desired
   3½ cups Buttercream
      Frosting (page 95)*

DECORATIONS & EQUIPMENT
   Assorted candies and
      sprinkles
   1 (19×13-inch) cake
      board, cut into 14×13-
      inch rectangle, if
      desired, and covered
   Heart-shaped cookie
      cutter
   Pastry bag and medium
      writing tip

1. Trim top and edges of cake. Cut as shown in diagram 1.

2. Position pieces on prepared cake board as shown in diagram 2, connecting with some of the yellow frosting.

3. Frost entire cake with Base Frosting to seal in crumbs.

4. Frost again with yellow frosting. Decorate neck with assorted candies.

5. Using cookie cutter, make outline on T-shirt; fill with sprinkles. Using wooden pick, write "Happy Birthday" as shown in photo.

6. Using writing tip and red frosting, pipe outline of heart and letters.
   Makes 14 to 16 servings

*Color 3 cups frosting yellow and ½ cup red.

CAKE & FROSTINGS
1 (9-inch) round cake
1 cup Base Frosting
    (page 94), if desired
2 cups Buttercream
    Frosting (page 95)*

DECORATIONS & EQUIPMENT
2 black licorice candies or
    jelly beans
1 red licorice whip
1 (10-inch) round cake
    board, covered, or
    large plate
Pastry bag and medium
    writing tip

1. Trim top of cake. Place on prepared cake board.

2. Frost entire cake with Base Frosting to seal in crumbs.

3. Frost again with blue frosting.

4. Using writing tip and white frosting, pipe 4 concentric circles, about 1 inch apart, and a dot in the center of the cake. Using spatula or tip of knife, draw through circles at regular intervals as shown in photo below, *alternating direction each time.*

5. Place candies for spider's body and head on cake. Cut 8 licorice whip pieces; curve and arrange for legs.

Makes 10 to 12 servings

***Color 1½ cups frosting blue; reserve ½ cup white frosting.**

Variation: *Can also be made as a 2-layer cake. Use two 9-inch round cakes and increase blue frosting to 2½ cups; decorate as above.*

Play a game of spiderwebs with the children at this party. You'll need a ball of colored yarn for each child at the party. (It is easier to play if there is a different color for each child.) Before the party begins, tie a prize to the end of each ball of yarn and hide the prize. Then unwind the balls of yarn all around a room—around the furniture, under tables, behind the sofa—creating a spiderweb of colored yarn. When the party starts, pass out the loose ends of yarn to the children. Have them wind the yarn back up into a ball, following it all around the room until they find the prize.

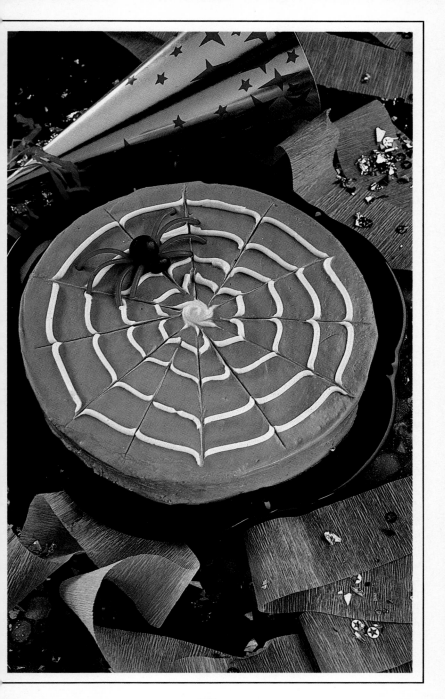

Wuzzy the Bear

CAKES & FROSTINGS
2 (9-inch) round cakes
1 recipe Jam Glaze
   (page 94), if desired
2¼ cups Chocolate
   Buttercream Frosting
   (page 95)
1¼ cups Buttercream
   Frosting (page 95)*

DECORATIONS & EQUIPMENT
Chocolate sprinkles
Assorted candies
2 large yellow gumdrops
1 large red gumdrop
1 (19×13-inch) cake
   board, cut into 13×13-
   inch square and
   covered

1. Trim tops of cakes; place one cake on prepared cake board. Cut remaining cake as shown in diagram 1.

2. Position pieces on prepared cake board as shown in diagram 2, connecting with some of the chocolate frosting.

3. Brush cake lightly with Jam Glaze. Let dry 1 hour.

4. Using wooden pick, draw 4-inch circle for face as shown in photo. Frost bear, except for face and bow tie, with chocolate frosting; sprinkle with chocolate sprinkles.

5. Frost face with white frosting. Frost bow tie with blue frosting and decorate with assorted candies as shown.

6. Roll out gumdrops for eyes and tongue.**

7. Decorate face as shown, using frosting to attach eyes, nose and tongue, if needed.
   Makes 12 to 16 servings

Color ¾ cup frosting blue; reserve ½ cup white frosting.

**See tip on rolling gumdrops, page 28.*

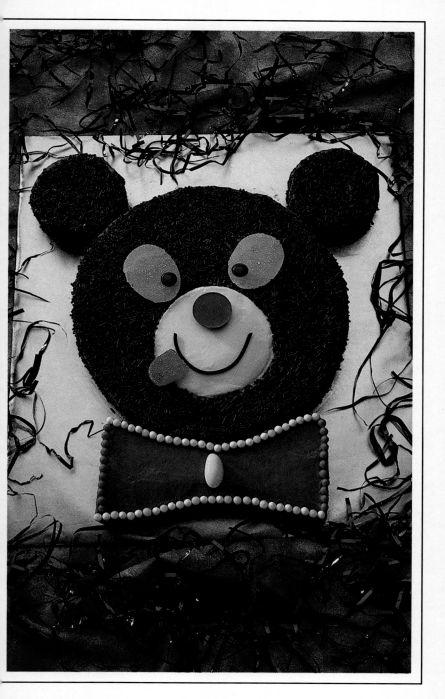

Basic cakes & frostings

Use the following baking times when preparing any of the cakes in this chapter:

- 1 (13×9-inch) cake: 35 to 40 minutes
- 1 (10-inch) Bundt® cake : 45 to 55 minutes
- 2 (9-inch) cakes: 35 to 40 minutes
- 2 (8-inch) squares: 30 to 35 minutes
- 3 (8-inch) rounds: 20 to 25 minutes
- 8 large (4-inch) cupcakes: 35 to 40 minutes
- 24 medium (2¾-inch) cupcakes: 20 to 25 minutes

White cake

2¼ cups all-purpose flour
1 tablespoon baking powder
½ teaspoon salt
1⅔ cups sugar
½ cup butter or margarine, softened
1 cup milk
2 teaspoons vanilla
3 egg whites

Preheat oven to 350°F. Grease and flour cake pan(s) or grease and line with waxed paper. Sift flour, baking powder and salt together in large bowl. Stir in sugar. Add butter, milk and vanilla; beat with electric mixer at low speed 30 seconds. Beat at medium speed 2 minutes. Add egg whites; beat 2 minutes. Pour into prepared cake pan(s) and bake as directed above, until wooden pick inserted into center comes out clean. Cool in pan 10 minutes. Loosen cake edge from pan, invert on a rack, remove waxed paper and cool completely.

YELLOW BUTTER CAKE

- 2 cups all-purpose flour
- 4 teaspoons baking powder
- ½ teaspoon salt
- 1½ cups sugar
- ½ cup butter or margarine, softened
- 1 cup milk
- 1 teaspoon vanilla
- 3 eggs

Preheat oven to 350°F. Grease and flour cake pan(s) or grease and line with waxed paper. Sift flour, baking powder and salt together in large bowl. Stir in sugar. Add butter, milk and vanilla and beat with electric mixer at low speed 30 seconds. Beat at medium speed 2 minutes. Add eggs; beat 2 minutes. Pour into prepared cake pan(s) and bake as directed on page 92, until wooden pick inserted into center comes out clean. Cool in pan 10 minutes. Loosen cake edge from pan, invert on a rack, remove waxed paper and cool completely.

CHOCOLATE CAKE

- 2 cups all-purpose flour
- ⅔ cup unsweetened cocoa powder
- 1¾ teaspoons baking soda
- ½ teaspoon baking powder
- ½ teaspoon salt
- 1¾ cups sugar
- ⅔ cup shortening
- 1 cup cold water
- 2 teaspoons vanilla
- 3 eggs

Preheat oven to 350°F. Grease and flour cake pan(s) or grease and line with waxed paper. Sift flour, cocoa, baking soda, baking powder and salt together in large bowl. Stir in sugar. Add shortening. Gradually beat in water at low speed with electric mixer until combined. Stir in vanilla. Beat at high speed 2 minutes. Add eggs; beat 2 minutes. Pour into prepared cake pan(s) and bake as directed on page 92, until wooden pick inserted into center comes out clean. Cool in pan 10 minutes. Loosen cake edge from pan, invert on a rack, remove waxed paper and cool completely.

Base Frosting

**3 cups powdered sugar,
   sifted
½ cup butter or margarine,
   softened
¼ cup milk
½ teaspoon vanilla**

Combine powdered sugar,
butter, milk and vanilla in large
bowl. Beat with electric mixer
until smooth. Add more milk, 1
teaspoon at a time. Frosting
should be fairly thin.

Makes about 2 cups

Light & Fluffy Frosting

**2 egg whites*
⅔ cup sugar
5 tablespoons light corn
   syrup
Dash salt
1 teaspoon vanilla**

Combine egg whites, sugar,
corn syrup and salt in top of
double boiler or stainless steel
bowl. Set over boiling water.
Beat constantly with electric
mixer until stiff peaks form,
about 7 minutes. Remove from
water and beat in vanilla.

Makes about 2 cups

*Use clean, uncracked eggs

Uncooked Fondant

**¼ cup butter or margarine,
   softened
4 cups powdered sugar,
   sifted
¼ cup evaporated milk
1 teaspoon vanilla**

Beat butter in medium bowl until
light and fluffy. Gradually beat in
powdered sugar. Beat in milk
and vanilla. Knead on surface
sprinkled with additional
powdered sugar until smooth
and glossy. Divide in portions,
knead in paste color and shape
as desired. Uncooked fondant
can be well wrapped and
refrigerated overnight or frozen
several weeks. Bring to room
temperature before using.

Makes about 1 cup

Jam Glaze

**1 cup apricot or seedless
   raspberry jam
1 tablespoon water**

Bring jam and water to a boil in
small saucepan. Remove from
heat. Cool before using. Spread
over cake and let stand about 1
hour before frosting.

Makes about 1 cup

Note: *Use apricot jam if the
cake is being covered by a
light frosting. The raspberry jam
is particularly good with
chocolate cake and frosting.*

Buttercream Frosting

6 cups powdered sugar, sifted and divided
¾ cup butter or margarine, softened
¼ cup shortening
6 to 8 tablespoons milk, divided
1 teaspoon vanilla

Combine 3 cups powdered sugar, butter, shortening, 4 tablespoons milk and vanilla in large bowl. Beat with electric mixer until smooth. Add remaining powdered sugar; beat until light and fluffy, adding more milk, 1 tablespoon at a time, as needed for good spreading consistency.

Makes about 3½ cups

Chocolate Buttercream Frosting

6 cups powdered sugar, sifted and divided
1 cup butter or margarine, softened
4 to 6 squares (1 ounce each) unsweetened chocolate, melted and cooled slightly
8 to 10 tablespoons milk, divided
1 teaspoon vanilla

Combine 3 cups powdered sugar, butter, melted chocolate, to taste, 6 tablespoons milk and vanilla in large bowl. Beat with electric mixer until smooth. Add remaining powdered sugar; beat until light and fluffy, adding more milk, 1 tablespoon at a time, as needed for good spreading consistency.

Makes about 3½ cups

SKILL LEVEL INDEX